HOPE

FOR

A

HURTING

HEART

a little book of hope and self-care

Gently Spoken Communications

DEDICATED TO

THE PEOPLE WHO

OPENED THE DOOR TO

SOMETHING DIFFERENT

AND TENDERLY WALKED

INTO MY HEART.

"EVERY EXPERIENCE

GOD GIVES US,

EVERY PERSON

HE PUTS IN OUR LIVES,

IS THE PERFECT

PREPARATION FOR THE

FUTURE IN WHICH ONLY

HE CAN SEE."

AUTHOR UNKNOWN

I have learned that we grieve many losses in our lives.

This book is about my first experience with the kind of grief that felt devastating to me. It is also the story of what I learned from my loss and how I evolved from it. I share this story with you because—for some reason—others have found it helpful. It is the story I have been asked to tell at churches and community groups, in schools and to women's groups.

And when they see who I am today, it seems to inspire them and encourage them.

I am not implying that breaking up with your first love or making a move that takes you far from family and friends is equal in consequence to losing a child or divorcing after 25 years. What I am saying is that it feels that way. At least, at first.

So here is my story.

Along the way I have gathered some precious touchstones of wisdom. Some are from my own experience. Some are what I learned by watching and listening to others. With their blessing, I have included pieces of their stories as well.

I hope they affirm you, encourage you, and—in time—help you to soar.

Cheryl

TODAY I WILL GIVE MYSELF A BIG HUG

I was a vivacious and spirited woman. Many people envied my spontaneity, freedom and optimism in the face of risks. I had lived in foreign countries and traveled to exotic places. I owned my own business—one I had started—and thrived on the autonomy it gave me. I chased dreams and flourished as they came true. And I was in love with a charming, handsome man.

To make matters sweeter still, I was surrounded by a loving family and friends. In fact it was to them that I freely gave advice. Even when they didn't ask for it.

You see, I thought I knew how to "do life."

Then suddenly, my world went dark. Without warning, my relationship with that charming, handsome man—the one I believed to be the love of my life—ended abruptly.

So very abruptly.

I AM A COMPASSIONATE AND LOVING PERSON

All those things people say about having the wind knocked out of you are true. Abandoned and reeling, I found myself under an avalanche of grief. No words comforted me. I would lie in bed each morning and grasp for the shattered pieces of my heart. I tried to will it whole again. But I couldn't. I didn't know how—let alone where—to begin.

Worse yet, I felt out of control. A dark tunnel stretched before me. Without air. Without any way out, I cried myself to sleep each night and woke each morning hugging a tear-soaked pillow. And that spirited, vivacious woman I had come to expect in the mirror? Even she had left me hopeless and alone.

My bedroom floor, covered with books on loss, grief and self-esteem, reflected my search for answers... "Why me Lord? Will I ever be happy again? How do I end this heartache?"

TODAY I WILL ASK FOR HELP

I had difficulty getting out of bed. The thought of going to work was overwhelming. After all, I didn't want people to see me like this. I was so sad, so very, incredibly, sad.

But the reality was—I had no choice.

As the sole employee of my gift shop, my responsibilities hadn't come to an end simply because my life had. And so I unlocked the doors each day and tried to greet each customer with a smile.

But the change in me was too great to hide. My regular customers were the first to notice. They missed the light in my eyes, the playfulness in my step. Puzzled and concerned, they dared to ask, "Are you okay?"

It was not what I expected. And it was a tenderness I couldn't refuse. Disarmed by their genuine concern, I opened my heart. I told them why I hurt. And when they reached out, I—literally— fell into their arms.

I AM RICH IN HOPE AND SPIRIT

They held me with their understanding. They embraced my sadness as their own. And they shared their own stories, stories of loss and heartbreak. They talked about the loss of a spouse. The tragic loss of a child. Sister. Brother. Mother or Father.

They talked about other losses too... a career ended without explanation; the diagnosis we so dread; the elusiveness of hope; the vulnerability of faith; the loss of a dream.

I no longer felt alone.

I felt as if God had surrounded me with guardian angels, human angels who took me under their wings and helped me believe better days would come. Ironically, these angels were also my customers who came to me looking for a gift.

I AM GRATEFUL FOR ALL THE BLESSINGS IN MY LIFE

Instead, THEY were the givers and the gift was mine... the gift of hope.

In time, the ache in me subsided. My broken heart began to mend in spite of my certainty that it would never be whole again. And as I emerged—a little wiser, undeniably stronger—so did my business.

There was a new focus, a new clarity to the purpose with which I stocked my shelves. I was drawn to messages and merchandise that affirmed people as worthy and deserving. I sought out gifts that nurtured the heart and touched lives with the hope of healing and of growth.

It was as if my entire world was new, RE-created from the inside out. And I had a mission. It became my passion to create a place of sanctuary and serenity for others who were in need of hope and healing. I wanted to give back to others what my customers, my family and my friends had so generously given to me.

I AM GRATEFUL FOR ALL THE LESSONS I HAVE LEARNED

Before this encounter with loss, if someone had told me that—sometimes—we need brokenness in order to become whole again, I would not have understood. But experience is a gifted teacher. And this is what I learned…

 I learned that feelings of grief and loss are part of everyone's life. No one escapes them. And while we can't control these experiences, it is one of life's great discoveries that we can make choices about how to deal with them.

 I found out—to my great surprise—that loss of one kind often becomes a lightening rod for other, earlier losses. At first, I was puzzled by the magnitude of my grief over a lost love. After all, I knew people who had suffered multiple deaths in a single day. In comparison, mine was a relatively small tragedy; and yet—I was completely undone.

TODAY I WILL LIVE WITH HOPE IN MY HEART

Then I began to remember…the death of my father years before. The death of my nephew. These were profound losses to me. They were also ones that I had not been ready–or willing–to grieve earlier. I think I was afraid they would hurt too much. And I was right.

Which was the beginning of my next discovery: THERE IS NO SUBSTITUTE FOR GRIEVING. Nor is there an easy way out. We may think that burying feelings we don't know quite what to do with will make them go away. But then–one day–something stirs that reservoir and without warning all that raw emotion we had forgotten erupts like a volcano. Fiercely. Uncontrollably. And we begin to wonder if we'll ever emerge from the ruins or savor the sunshine again.

I AM ENOUGH JUST THE WAY I AM

I learned that where there's grief in abundance, depression isn't far behind. The trouble is a person living with depression is often the last one to recognize it. If you experience repeated bouts of hopelessness or your sadness becomes an Arctic winter in duration, depression is at work. Seeking professional help—whether from a family doctor, a psychologist, a spiritual director or the clergy, can be sunshine to someone who only sees darkness. Your life is much too worthy and precious to live forever in sadness. Be willing to ask for help if you need it.

I learned that significant loss often includes a "loss of self". Many of us travel through life validating our self-worth through relationships, jobs and external sources that include everything from prestige to possessions. But WE are not these things. Each of us is an individual, unique and unrepeatable. EACH DAY we need to affirm how worthy we are, simply for who we are.

TODAY I WILL LOVE AND HONOR MYSELF

I came to understand that no matter how much you love someone, you cannot control anyone else's life, his or her health or the decisions they make. You can, however, take charge of your own life. Learning to love yourself and respect your needs will help you become strong again—both physically and emotionally.

I learned that we can choose to reach out and accept the help people offer us, or we can push them away.

I learned (and this one took me awhile) that we can remain stuck in the past and anxious about the future. Or, we can try to live in the present moment... one hour and one day at a time.

I discovered firsthand why Let Go and Let God has given so many others the courage to face another day. Although letting go is one of life's most difficult challenges, it is also one of life's most liberating lessons. I made a wonderful discovery in the book, A Course of Love by Mary Perron and Dan Odegard. Put simply: have the grace to give up what has been FOR WHAT COULD BE.

TODAY I WILL TRY AND DO ONE THING
THAT WILL MAKE A POSITIVE IMPACT
ON MY LIFE

꩜ I learned that WE CAN BECOME BETTER OR WE CAN BECOME BITTER. I have my friend Esther to thank for this wisdom. After hearing her story about the loss of a young child, I know what choice she made. You can see it in her eyes and feel it in her kind, compassionate heart. With her story to inspire me, I began to see that I really did have choices—even when it felt like there weren't any. Some days that choice was as simple as changing my attitude or surrendering my grief to a higher power.

꩜ I learned I could choose to take baby steps toward healing or I could get lost in self-pity (and miss for all time the wonder of a sunrise or the comfort of coffee with a friend).

꩜ And, most importantly, I have learned:

WE ARE ALL WORTHY AND DESERVING
OF LOVE IN OUR LIVES.

Watch for it! Love comes to us in many different ways...through a friend, a child, a sibling, a parent, a grandparent, an aunt, an uncle, a pet, or God.

TODAY I WILL BEGIN TO BELIEVE IN MYSELF. AGAIN.

So now the question is:

What can you do to make this challenging time in your life a little less painful? What can you do to be kinder and gentler to yourself?

Here is what I will hold dear the next time loss invades my life. I offer it humbly and hopefully:

♥ Give yourself permission to experience all of those feelings you don't know what to do with. There is nothing wrong with you. You have faced a great loss and need time to heal.

♥ Surround yourself with people who make you feel good about yourself. Seek out and nurture friendships that are positive and encouraging.

I AM SO MUCH MORE THAN MY BODY.
I AM SPIRIT, I AM HEART.

♥ Observe and become aware of how nature's gifts keep RE-generating around you. Trees lose their leaves in the fall and new buds appear in the spring. Flowers die off only to bloom again and again. Caterpillars turn into magnificent butterflies. Watch and listen. You, too, will once again thrive and grow.

♥ Eavesdrop on your "self-talk". Negative, disparaging, and hopeless thoughts only erode the spirit. Determine to replace them with positive affirmations.

"EVERY DAY IN EVERY WAY I
GET BETTER AND BETTER AND BETTER."

"I AM A WORTHY AND DESERVING PERSON."

"TODAY, I WILL LIVE IN THE PRESENT MOMENT."

This may take some practice, but don't give up. Most good things do!

Today I will give myself permission to be sad

♥ Forgive yourself for everything you did—and didn't—do! Learn to accept yourself as one big, lovable, imperfect and perfectly human being.

♥ Congratulate yourself on making it through another day! Buy yourself a treat. Give yourself a hug. Spend time doing something you love. You deserve it.

♥ Treat yourself as you would your own best friend. Talk to yourself with love, praise and encouragement. (After all, who knows better than you the person you are affirming?)

♥ Read and listen to other people's stories of loss. Not only will you discover that you are not alone, but their stories will help you take heart. Don't be surprised if they even help you recognize new strength, and courage in yourself.

TODAY I WILL MAKE A LIST OF ALL THE THINGS I ENJOY DOING.
MAYBE I WILL TRY AND DO ONE OF THEM.

♥ Get busy! Exercise. Go back to work. Take a class. It will get your mind engaged—or at least distracted! Reach out and help others through volunteering. Your kindness will come back to you in countless ways.

♥ Keep a gratitude journal. Each day, spend a few moments jotting down something you are grateful for:

A SPECIAL FRIEND

A PRAYER ANSWERED

MAKING IT THROUGH THE NIGHT

A BEAUTIFUL SUNSET

CLEAN SHEETS

A FLOWER

A SMILE

A PHONE CALL

Putting your thoughts and feelings on paper is healing. One day you will be able to look back and see how far you have come.

TODAY I WILL HAVE TRUST AND FAITH IN THE UNKNOWN

♥ KNOW that you are a somebody—no matter your age, your marital status, your education, or your income.

You are a SOMEBODY, a very important and worthy somebody. You are a gift to this world with a unique purpose and life all your own.

No one can take away your history, your memories, your pain, your joy and all the ways in which your life here has so beautifully touched others. It is yours!   Recognize and CELEBRATE how special you are.

You are a Survivor. You are a kind and loving person, a gift of God, and a very important SOMEBODY. No one, absolutely no one can take your magnificence away.

I AM NEVER ALONE

Our lives, like stories, have a beginning, a middle and an ending. Once I felt as if mine was over. And it is true that loss marks the end of something dear. But (and here's the most amazing part) it is not the end of YOUR story—your very own, irrepressible, still-in-the-works life story.

And the loss that started me on this journey? There is still an ache. There always will be.

But I continue to grow because of it. And, best of all, I don't have to grow alone! Family and friends are living reminders of the support and encouragement by which we mend broken hearts and fill empty places.

One spring morning remains vivid in my mind.

TODAY I WILL SURRENDER MY GRIEF TO A HIGHER POWER

Particularly consumed by my sadness, I sat curled up in a chair sobbing when my mother walked into the room. She gently placed her arms around me and tenderly whispered in my ear, "Don't worry, God just has a different plan for you."

Today, I look back at that moment many years ago, and I am in awe of her wisdom and her knowing. Whenever I am in doubt about my life, those wise words have a way of slipping back into my mind.

Please, don't give up HOPE.

Have faith.
Have trust.
Have patience.

God has a plan for you, too.

My wise and precious mother told me so.

Today I will spend quiet time in prayer and / or meditation

LITTLE STORIES
OF
HOPE
AND
SELF-CARE

TODAY I WILL CURL UP IN A BLANKET
AND READ A REALLY GOOD BOOK

At the age of 49, Kathy still finds comfort in stroking something soft and fuzzy—a buttery soft stuffed animal—that was with her during a family crisis and the subsequent death of her father. Today, that same stuffed animal not only reminds her of her losses, it also reminds her that she is a Survivor.

Ohrn, who lost his beloved wife after 55 years of marriage, brings delight to his neighbors every spring. He tends his garden of colorful tulips with passion and brings the joy of renewal and beauty to an entire community.

TODAY I WILL DO SOMETHING NICE FOR MYSELF

G ene was middle aged when the crisis hit his long-term marriage. Out of the self doubt and rejection, he began sharing his pain with people who were important to him. To his amazement, an outpouring of love and support followed—and with it, the courage to face an uncertain future.

D ivorced, Lucy joined a women's support group where she met others who could empathize with her situation. After a time of healing, Lucy the Conservative, became Lucy the Risk Taker. She left the comfort of family and friends in the suburbs, moved to the city and never looked back.

TODAY I WILL GIVE MYSELF PERMISSION TO BE HAPPY

Darlene, who has lost a child, battled cancer and today lives with congestive heart failure, lives optimistically. When asked how she maintains such a positive attitude, she replied, "Whenever I begin to feel sorry for myself, I think of all the people in the world who have much greater problems and hardships."

Gina finds comfort in quiet moments. After she puts her three boys to bed, she likes to draw a warm bath filled with lots of bubbles, read an inspirational book, pray and meditate.

TODAY I WILL TAKE A WALK AMONG THE TREES

At the age of 58, Julia felt alone after her best friend, her husband, died. Although many of her "couple" friends would continue to include her in activities, she often felt like a third or fifth person. Julia's life changed dramatically after she met Marion, also a widow. Together they travel to the local theater for an afternoon matinee or as far away as Nova Scotia for a new experience.

During a painful divorce, Barb began weekly visits to the local florist to have fresh flowers refilled in her small vase. The flowers symbolize a new beginning for Barb and remind her that life can be filled with beauty and wonder.

Today I will begin to live in the present moment

Friday nights were difficult for Beth following the break up of a serious relationship. After all Friday was date night. Realizing this, one Friday night, a caring friend invited her to go horseback riding. Fridays became a standing engagement at the ranch. Beth renewed her passion for riding as well as her spirit through contact with the natural beauty that surrounded her.

After the death of her husband, Jeri became a hospice volunteer. Later she went on to volunteer at a local elementary school where she helps first graders with their reading. Today at the age of 79, she works at a gift shop at least two days per week and has become Main Street's favorite mom.

GRANT ME THE GRACE TO
EMBRACE MY LIFE

Growing up, Nora lived in several different countries. Change became a way of life and new situations proved an endless source of interest. But when the last of Nora's three children left home, she was totally unprepared for the avalanche of loneliness that followed. To her surprise, it was the solitude of a nearby nature center that provided comfort. To this day when she feels lonely, Nora finds solace in nature and long walks among the trees.

Duty isn't a word we hear much today. But for Darren it was heartfelt duty that helped him survive a time of betrayal and extreme pain. For him, the countermeasure for overwhelming chaos was hope in spiritual—rather than material—outcomes. "Life as we know it is pretty temporary. But eternity's forever. Remember who you are and that YOU ARE LOVED."

THE FOLLOWING PAGES ARE RESERVED FOR
PERSONAL THOUGHTS AND AFFIRMATIONS

WAYS IN WHICH I CAN BE KINDER AND
GENTLER WITH MYSELF:

THINGS I HAVE TO LOOK FORWARD TO:

THINGS I AM GRATEFUL FOR:

ONE LAST LESSON
A NOTE FROM THE AUTHOR

For a long time I hesitated to publish Hope for a Hurting Heart. And rightly so. Exposing my innermost thoughts and revisiting painful ground is more vulnerable than I care to be most days.

I also questioned the significance of my pain when compared to others whose loss seemed to be much greater. What did I have to say that could grace their lives with hope?

Dear friends thought otherwise. The circumstances that plunge us into grief are all worthy of validation, they reminded me. And the multitude of ways in which we grieve? They are matched by a thousand ways in which we learn to take—and give—comfort along the way. And so I began to put my hurt—and heart—on paper.

Thanks to an entire team of caring, compassionate cheer-leaders—family and friends—their words of encouragement and kind acts of support, this book moved from my heart into your hands. I thank all of you who cheered me on, especially during those times when it felt as if there was nothing in life to cheer about. Today, I treasure life, and most of all I treasure all of you.

Also, a most heartfelt thanks to all the individuals who trusted me enough to share their stories, my editors, Suzanne Foust and Margie Adler and to my dear artist friend, Sandy Fougner. And lastly, a special HEART-FULL of gratitude to my amazing mother, Julia C. Karpen, for always, always believing.

Cheryl Karpen

BLESSINGS

OTHER BOOKS BY CHERYL KARPEN:

To Let You Know I Care
Can We Try Again?

For more information contact:
Gently Spoken Communications
Tele. # 763-506-9933
gentlyspoken.com
or write to us at:
Gently Spoken Communications
P.O. Box 245
Anoka, Mn. 55303

Hope for a Hurting Heart
Copyright November 2000, Cheryl Karpen